DOING FAITH RIGHT

YOU CAN BE FULLY PERSUADED

GARY KEESEE

Doing Faith Right: You can be Fully Persuaded
Copyright © 2022 by Gary Keesee.

Unless otherwise noted, all Scriptures quotations are taken from the New International Version® (NIV)® of the Holy Bible. Copyright © 1973, 1978, 1984, 2011 by Biblica, Inc.™ All rights reserved worldwide.

Scripture quotations marked (BSB) are taken from the Berean Study Bible. Copyright © 2016, 2020 by Bible Hub. All rights reserved worldwide.

Scripture quotations marked (EHV) are taken from the English Heritage Version® of the Holy Bible. Copyright © 2019 by the Wartburg Project, Inc. All rights reserved.

Scripture quotations marked (ESV) are taken from the English Standard Version® of the Holy Bible. Text Edition: 2016. Copyright © 2001 by Crossway, a publishing ministry of Good News Publishers. All rights reserved.

Printed in the United States of America. All rights reserved under International Copyright Law. Contents and/or cover may not be reproduced in whole or in part in any form without the express written consent of the Publisher.

ISBN: 978-1-958486-37-5

Published by Free Indeed Publishing.
Distributed by Faith Life Now.

Faith Life Now
P.O. Box 779
New Albany, OH 43054
1-(888)-391-LIFE

You can reach Faith Life Now Ministries on the Internet at www.faithlifenow.com.

CONTENTS

CHAPTER ONE:
What Is Faith?..05

CHAPTER TWO:
Why Is Faith Needed?.......................................09

CHAPTER THREE:
How Do We Get Faith?......................................21

CHAPTER FOUR:
How Do You Know If You Are Actually *in* Faith?....49

CHAPTER FIVE:
Understand Satan's Counterattack......................65

CHAPTER ONE
WHAT IS FAITH?

Faith is a term that Christians throw around loosely. And I am convinced that many, if not the majority, do not know what faith is, why it is needed, how to know if they are in faith, and how to find faith. If faith is the switch that healed the woman in Matthew 9:20-22, as Jesus stated, then we need to take a very close look at faith! We find our definition of faith in Romans 4:18-21. Oh, I know what you are thinking, *No, Gary. Hebrews 11:1 is our definition of faith.*

> *Faith is being sure about what we hope for, being convinced about things we do not see.*
> —Hebrews 11:1 (EHV)

Yes, that is the traditional answer, but if you look at the Scripture, Hebrews 11:1 is telling us the benefits of faith, not what faith actually is. I believe our Scripture in Romans will give us a very clear picture of what faith actually is.

> *Against all hope, Abraham in hope believed and so became the father of many nations,*

> *just as it had been said to him, "So shall your offspring be." Without weakening in his faith, he faced the fact that his body was as good as dead—since he was about a hundred years old—and that Sarah's womb was also dead. Yet he did not waver through unbelief regarding the promise of God, but was strengthened in his faith and gave glory to God, <u>being fully persuaded</u> that God had power to do what he had promised.*
> —Romans 4:18-21

Let's understand the setting of this story. Abraham and Sarah could not have children. I do not mean they were having trouble conceiving a child and should keep trying. I mean they were almost 100 years of age, and it was over. Their bodies could not have children; it was impossible! Yet God promised Abraham a child even though in the natural it was utterly impossible. The Bible says that Abraham was fully persuaded that God had the power to do what He said, in spite of the natural facts that stated a different story.

Here then is our definition of faith: "being fully persuaded that God has the power to do what He has promised." I state it this way: **being in agreement with heaven**, not just mentally but fully persuaded, our hearts settled and convinced totally of what God has said, in spite of the natural realm indicating something else.

Our definition of what faith is:
Faith is being fully persuaded of what God says! It is our hearts and minds being in agreement with heaven, our hearts being fully persuaded, confident, and at rest.

CHAPTER TWO
WHY IS FAITH NEEDED?

Why can't God just heal everyone in the hospital when He wants to? Why can't He stop wars? Why can't He send angels to preach the Gospel to us? I am sure you have heard all of these questions before. The answer is that He can't. It is not that God does not have the ability to do so. He does not have the jurisdiction or the authority to do so. "Gary, are you saying that God can't do whatever He wants to do?" I know this sounds really strange to you right now, but let's look at the Bible to find our answer to that one.

> But there is a place where someone has testified:
>
> > "What is mankind that you are mindful of them, a son of man that you care for them? You made them a little lower than the angels; you crowned them with glory and honor and put everything under their feet."
>
> In putting everything under them, God left nothing that is not subject to them. Yet at

> *present we do not see everything subject to them.*
>
> —Hebrews 2:6-8

We can see from this Scripture that God gave man complete legal jurisdiction over the entire earth realm when he was placed here. There was nothing that was not under his jurisdiction. He ruled over this realm with absolute jurisdiction and authority. His ability to rule with authority was backed up by the government which had set him here. In essence, he ruled with the delegated authority of the Kingdom of God. He wore the crown of that government, which represented the glory of God, the anointing, and the position of honor that he bore.

To get a good picture of what this looks like, think of a natural king. Although he is a natural man and bears no real power in his natural being, he wears a crown that signifies he stands in representation of not only himself but also an entire kingdom and government. His words carry authority only because they are backed up by all the power and natural resources of the government and kingdom he represents.

If you think of a sheriff directing traffic, he will stop a massive tractor-trailer truck with a command, "Stop in the name of the law." Yes, the truck is much bigger than the man, and the man, in himself, is no match for the truck, but the truck stops. It stops not because of the man but because of the badge the man wears, which represents a government.

In this case, the government is much bigger than the man who wears the badge. For the truck driver, there is no fear of the man, but there is a fear of the government that the man represents, causing the truck to stop.

The same is true here. Adam ruled over everything that was created in the earth realm. God's power and dominion, represented by the crown of glory and honor, gave man the assurance that his words ruled on behalf of the Kingdom of God.

CHAPTER TWO: Why Is Faith Needed?

It is very important to note that when Adam lost his ability to rule over the earth by committing treason against God's government, he lost his crown. The earth realm became tainted and changed. Death entered the earth realm, and Satan then had a legal claim of authority and influence in the affairs of men.

It is imperative that you also understand that man is still the legal ruler over the earth realm, as God has placed him in that position, but he now has no authority to rule spiritually as he once had. Even in his fallen state, however, he is still in charge of the earth. Yes, he no longer has his crown of God's government to back him up. He has no authority to rule with God's power and glory; he has lost his position of honor. But he is still the only legal door to the earth realm. This is why God has to use Spirit-filled people to bring about His will in the lives of men.

In the same way, Satan uses demon-inspired people to affect the earth realm toward his plan for man. This principle of man's jurisdiction over the earth is vital to your understanding of Kingdom law, and once you understand it, it will answer many questions you may have in the future as to why certain things happen, or why certain things did or do not happen spiritually.

You may say, "But I thought God owned the earth and the fullness thereof?" True, He does. I hope the following example will help you understand what I am saying.

If I leased a home that I owned to you, although I legally owned the home, I legally gave up the right to drop by anytime I wanted to. There is a clause in most leases that specifies when landlords may legally enter rented premises—for example, to deal with an emergency or to make repairs—and the amount of notice required. If I tried to enter the home outside of this agreement, it would be considered breaking and entering, even if I owned the property. If I violated the law specified in the lease, I could then be legally forced to vacate the premises even though I owned it.

CHAPTER TWO: Why Is Faith Needed?

This illustrates why Satan had to go through Adam to gain access to the earth realm. Only Adam had the key! Satan had to go through the door, and Adam was it. If Satan tried to go around Adam, he would have legally been forced out.

> *The devil led him up to a high place and showed him in an instant all the kingdoms of the world. And he said to him, "I will give you all their authority and splendor, for it has been given to me, and I can give it to anyone I want to. So if you worship me, it will all be yours."*
>
> —Luke 4:5-7

You can see in this verse that Satan claims that the authority and splendor (wealth) of the kingdoms of men have been given to him. Who gave him this authority? The one who had it—Adam! Thus God cannot just burst into the affairs of men without going through a legal entrance. If He did, Satan would claim foul play. No, God would have to go through the same door that Satan used to bring His government and authority to bear in the earth, and that was a man. But was there such a man?

> *The Lord had said to Abram, "Go from your country, your people and your father's household and go to the land I will show you. I will make you into a great nation, and I will bless you; I will make your name great, and you will be a blessing. I will bless those who bless you, and whoever curses you I will curse; and <u>all peoples on earth will be blessed through you</u>."*
>
> *—Genesis 12:1-3*

Abraham is called the father of our faith because he is the man that opened the door of the earth realm to God whereby all nations on the earth would be blessed. Of course, when this verse speaks of the nations being blessed, it is speaking of Jesus Christ, who would later make a way for the government of God to once again have legal access to the earth realm through the faith of Abraham. Abraham's faith opened a legal doorway for heaven, which God locked permanently open by making a legal agreement (covenant) with Abraham and his seed or heirs.

Let me paraphrase what I am saying. The government of heaven can only gain its access into the earth realm through a man or a woman on the earth because they have legal jurisdiction there. That legality can only be accomplished if a man or woman is totally persuaded in their heart of what God says (faith).

Another way to say it is that heaven can only legally affect a man or woman in the earth realm who desires and chooses to come under God's dominion and authority. This would be the same principle that Satan used to gain access into the earth, using Adam to do so. He convinced Adam that God could not be trusted and brought Adam's heart out of agreement with God. Consequently, Adam chose to believe Satan and rejected God's authority.

This is the same principle that God would then use to bring His government and authority back into the earth realm through Abraham. Abraham believed God, and his agreement was counted by God as righteousness, meaning that the required legal agreement was there. This agreement by both parties, God and Abraham, allowed God to put a legal contract (a covenant) in place that secured heaven's access into the earth realm, BUT it is vital to note that this agreement only affected Abraham and his heirs. A sign of this covenant was given to all of Abraham's heirs, which was circumcision. Circumcision is the cutting off of the foreskin from the male penis. As a man planted his seed in a woman, his seed had to pass through that circumcised penis, which declared to Satan and the father and mother themselves that this child stood before heaven as an heir of that legal agreement that God and Abraham had put in place.

As we read previously, however, each man or woman, although having that legal agreement <u>available</u> to them, still had to fulfill the legal requirement of their own heart being fully persuaded of what God said to actually enjoy the personal benefits of that agreement that God and Abraham made. In essence, the

CHAPTER TWO: Why Is Faith Needed?

covenant ran the power lines to their house, but they still had to turn on the switch by personally believing and acting on the Word of God.

Okay, we now know what faith is and why faith is legally required. It is now imperative that we know how to get faith and how to know if we are in faith.

CHAPTER THREE
HOW DO WE GET FAITH?

ere is a clue: You can't pray for faith. Surprised? I thought so.

> *Consequently, faith comes from hearing the message, and the message is heard through the word about Christ.*
> —Romans 10:17

How does faith come by hearing the Word of God? Is that all there is to it? What is the process? Is just hearing the Word all it takes for faith to be developed in the human spirit?

To understand how faith comes and what Romans 10:17 is talking about, we can look to Mark chapter 4. If you throw your Bible up in the air, it should land open to Mark chapter 4; it is that important! Jesus said in Mark 4:13 that if you did not understand what He was teaching in this chapter, you would not be able to understand any other parable in the Bible. I would say that is pretty important!

Why is this chapter so important? It is because it tells us how heaven interfaces with the earth

CHAPTER THREE: How Do We Get Faith?

realm, how it gains legality, and where that takes place. Nothing is more important to your life than knowing what this whole chapter is talking about. "How does the Kingdom of God operate?" you may ask. Read Mark chapter 4! In this chapter, Jesus tells us three parables regarding how faith is produced in the human spirit, which as you know now, is a requirement for heaven to legally invade Earth.

The three stories in this chapter are the parable of the sower, the parable of the man scattering seed, and the story of the mustard seed.

Let's begin by first looking at the second story Jesus tells in Mark chapter 4, the story of the man scattering seed.

> *He also said, "This is what the Kingdom of God is like. A man scatters seed on the ground. Night and day, whether he sleeps or gets up, the seed sprouts and grows, though he does not know how. All by itself the soil produces grain—first the stalk, then the head, then the full kernel in the head.*

> *As soon as the grain is ripe, he puts the sickle to it, because the harvest has come."*
> —Mark 4:26-29

Before we jump into this passage, let's first define our terms. What is the seed Jesus is talking about, and what is the ground? Jesus actually defines those terms in the preceding parable of the sower in the same chapter. The seed is the Word of God, and the ground is the heart of man, or the spirit of man. So in this parable, using Jesus's own definition of those two words, we would say that Jesus is saying a man scatters the Word of God into his own heart. Then all by itself the soil, or the heart of man starts to produce faith (agreement with heaven) in the earth realm.

Before I go forward, it is critical that you remember what our definition of faith is: the heart of a man or woman fully persuaded of what heaven says. This passage says that although the man does not know how the process works, the Word that was sown into his heart begins to grow and produce agreement all by itself. This happens if he sleeps or is awake; it does not matter. The process continues. As the man keeps the Word in his heart, slowly his heart is coming into agreement with what heaven says, and faith is being produced.

Our Scripture reference in Mark chapter 4 tells us that the heart produces agreement through a process. The story tells us that at first when our heart receives the Word, faith begins to form. Jesus compares that phase to a sprout. The sprout then goes on and continues to grow and becomes a stalk. Eventually, the head forms on the stalk, but even at this late phase, there is no fruit, no agreement, and no change in the natural realm. Then Jesus says the process continues as the head then matures and produces mature grain.

When the process reaches that point, when the mature seed is in the head, agreement is there and faith is there, allowing the man or woman to harvest into the earth realm what heaven has planted in the heart of the man.

Now pay close attention. Let's review what actually happened. Heaven sows the Word of God into the earth realm, into the heart of a man or woman where agreement is needed. At that time, the man's heart is not in agreement with heaven yet, but a process begins to take place in the heart that brings the heart, all by itself, into agreement with what was sown. Jesus uses a great illustration to show us this process. Comparing this process to a farmer sowing seed and how the plant matures, Jesus gives us a picture of what faith looks like. In the natural realm, when the seed in the head is mature, it will look **EXACTLY** like the seed that was sown into the ground. Let me say that again.

When the seed that is in the head of the plant matures, it will look exactly—EXACTLY—like the seed that was sown into the ground.

Plant a corn plant, and the mature seed in the ear will match the seed that you planted. They are the same, look the same, and taste the same. You can't tell the difference between the two; they are identical. So let me paraphrase what Jesus is saying. When we hear the Word (Romans 10:17), we are actually scattering God's Word into our spirit men, our hearts. If we keep that Word in our hearts, it will mature; and when it is mature, the pictures in our hearts (the earth realm) will match what heaven says.

If we put it in different terms, we could say that as you sow a promise from heaven into your heart, it will slowly produce confidence of what God said all by itself. Eventually, your heart will be fully persuaded of what heaven says, and agreement will be there. For instance, if you are facing sickness, your circumstances in your body are speaking to you that you are sick. As you sow the Word of God that says that God has paid the price for your healing through what Jesus did, your heart slowly begins to become convinced of what God says all by itself.

When that word matures in your heart, the confidence that you are healed becomes what

you believe and say. No longer are you simply quoting what heaven says. Your heart is now firmly convinced. When you say, "I am healed," it is not a formula that you are quoting; rather, this is what you believe and know to be a fact. What heaven says has now become your own perception of reality.

This is why Hebrews 11:1 (EHV) says:

> *Faith is being sure about what we hope for, being convinced about things we do not see.*

There is a supernatural assurance of what heaven says when faith is there, yet there is still another step in the process.

The man now must put in his sickle to harvest, to bring into his actual realm of existence, what he is sure of in his heart.

> *As soon as the grain is ripe, **he puts the sickle to it**, because the harvest has come.*
> —Mark 4:29

CHAPTER THREE: How Do We Get Faith?

Notice that even though the heart is in agreement with heaven, and heaven's reality has become the man or woman's reality, no real change has yet occurred in the physical realm. Because man is the one who naturally has jurisdiction here in the earth, he is the one who must also release that authority of heaven into this realm. God can't do it without the man or woman. I can show you this in the next Scripture.

> *For with the heart one believes and is **justified**, and with the mouth one **confesses** and is saved.*
> —Romans 10:10 (ESV)

With the heart man believes the Word, producing faith, and is justified. Justify is a legal term meaning the administration of law. So when a man's heart is in agreement with heaven, and his heart is fully persuaded of what heaven says, he is justified. It is then legal for heaven to flow into his life, into the earth realm. But being justified alone does not release the power of God. Like a house that has the power run to the house from the power station, there is one more step—turning the switch on to release the power, and then the lights come on. Why? Because as Romans 10:10 points out, there is one more step after being justified.

A man or woman who stands before heaven and earth justified must then confess or act upon that agreement to actually release the power and anointing of God into the earth realm. Please read that Scripture again and again until you completely understand what I am saying. This is how it works! This is how heaven gains legality in the earth realm—the heart is the interface of heaven in the earth realm, and then our words and actions are the switches that actually release heaven's power. Please pay close attention to the second part of that verse again: We are the ones who must release heaven's authority here.

The concept of heaven waiting on a man or woman to, first of all, provide legality and, secondly, jurisdiction in the earth realm can

CHAPTER THREE: How Do We Get Faith?

be seen through what Jesus taught in Matthew 16:19 and Matthew 18:18.

> *I will give you the keys of the kingdom of heaven; whatever you bind on earth will be bound in heaven, and whatever you loose on earth will be loosed in heaven.*
> —Matthew 16:19

> *Truly, I say to you, whatever you bind on earth shall be bound in heaven, and whatever you loose on earth shall be loosed in heaven.*
> —Matthew 18:18 (ESV)

Jesus states in Matthew 16:19 that He is going to give the church the keys (authority) of the Kingdom of heaven in the earth realm. He said that whatsoever you bind on Earth, heaven will back up, and whatsoever you loose on Earth, heaven will back up. Again, think of a police officer; he has the authority, but the government has the power. The police officer holds the key or the authority of the government, as he was sworn in to be an agent of that government. What he says, the government backs up. Remember, only a man or woman has legal jurisdiction here, and thus only a man or woman can give heaven legal jurisdiction here.

There is one more very important point that you need to know about faith. Let me reference our Scripture in Mark chapter 4 again for a moment.

> *All by itself **the soil produces grain**—first the stalk, then the head, then the full kernel in the head.*
> —Mark 4:28

Remember, Jesus defined the soil mentioned in this parable as representing the heart of man, or the spirit of man, as I mentioned before. Notice where faith is produced; does that surprise you? It is not a product of heaven, as most people believe, but it is produced here in the earth realm and is a product of your heart. You cannot pray for it or ask God for it. Faith is not needed in heaven. We will not need agreement in heaven. No, it is only required here in the earth realm, and it can only occur in the hearts of men and women on the earth. As the parable in Mark 4 teaches, there is only one way to get it—by putting the Word of God in your heart and letting the process of agreement take place.

So if I need faith, what would I do? I would scatter the Word of God into my heart and let it grow until faith was there. That is the only way it comes.

Before I leave Mark 4, I want to talk about the sickle mentioned there again.

> *As soon as the grain is ripe,* ***he puts the sickle to it***, *because the harvest has come.*
> —Mark 4:29

I believe that most of the church world has not been taught how to use the sickle, meaning people have not been taught how to harvest what they need. The church in general has been taught how to give but not how to cultivate and harvest from the seed they have sown. Jesus is very specific in this verse, saying that when the harvest of our faith is available, WE must put in the sickle. Even though we may have done a great job of releasing our seed in faith, unless we know how to put in the sickle, there will be no harvest. Quite frankly, I knew nothing about this either until the Lord began teaching me how the Kingdom operated. Let me give you a few examples of what this looks like.

I was invited to speak at a church in Atlanta. It was a Wednesday night service, and the church was not that big, but that was fine with me. I just loved teaching people about the Kingdom. As I arrived at the church, I found it strange that the doors were locked and no one was there. It was ten minutes before service was to begin.

I heard a really loud truck behind me; it sounded like it had no muffler at all. As I looked over, I saw an old beat-up, broken-down pickup truck pulling into the alley behind the church. I thought nothing of it; after all, I was in downtown Atlanta. As I waited, a man

CHAPTER THREE: How Do We Get Faith?

came walking from behind the building and introduced himself as the pastor. He said he was sorry for being late, but his old truck would not start. He told me he had to start the truck by coasting downhill then, once getting up some speed, popping the clutch since the starter was inoperative. He said many times it would not start at all, and he would have to walk the five miles to the church.

As he went on telling me about his church, he told me that although he was the pastor of the church, the church's main function was to feed inner city people. They provided over 10,000 meals a month at that location.

As the pastor was speaking, I was getting upset. Here was a man of God who was feeding 10,000 people a month, and he did not even have a reliable car? He was the only picture of God that many of those people he fed would ever see. If they saw him barely making it, having to walk to church five miles on a 100-degree summer day, what confidence would they have that God could help them? I could take care of that. I had a fairly young car with 20,000 miles on it at home that I could give him. I told him of my plan and that I would send one of my staff down to Atlanta with the car. He, of course, was thrilled. I spent that night teaching him and his small church about the Kingdom of God and how it functioned in relation to money.

When I went home, I arranged for the car to be driven to Atlanta. When my staff member came to my house to pick up the car, I knew that I was making a spiritual transaction in heaven. I knew that as I released that car into the Kingdom of God, I could believe God for a vehicle that I would have need of as well. I am not a car person, meaning I am not really into cars. Some people are, but I am not. A car is just a tool to me. I like to have a nice car, of course, but I usually drive them until they need replaced.

When my staff member stopped by, I went out into my garage, and I laid my hands on that car and said, "Father, I release this car into the work of your ministry, and as I release this car, I receive back a car…." I hesitated. I know how

CHAPTER THREE: How Do We Get Faith?

specific the Kingdom of God is, and I knew that just the word "car" would not do. I also knew that I had to be specific and that Drenda and I needed to be in agreement concerning the specifics of what we received. As I stood there mid-sentence, I also realized that I had no idea what kind of car I wanted. So I started over, "Lord, today I release this car into your ministry, and I believe that I receive a really nice car as I sow, but I will have to get back to you on the model and type when I figure that out." That was it; the car was gone. I really did not have any car in mind that I could say, "Yes, I want THAT car."

A few months went by. Drenda was in agreement with me in giving the car away, of course, and, like me, she did not have a clue what kind of car she wanted. Over the next two months, we talked about cars, and finally one day she said, "You know, I think I would enjoy having a convertible." I told her that I agreed and said I thought that sounded fun, but what kind? Again, we did not even know what kind of convertibles were out there.

But one day as we were driving out to lunch, my wife suddenly said, "That's it!" "What's it?" I said. "That's it," she said as she was pointing across the parking lot of the restaurant we had pulled into. "What's it?" I said. "That car, that's the car I want!" I then saw a sharp convertible across the parking lot. "Let's go see what kind it is," I said. So we drove over to the car and pulled up behind it. Well, no wonder we liked it. It was a BMW 645Ci, a nice convertible for sure, and a very expensive one at that.

To be honest with you, when I saw that make of car, I thought, "Okay, Lord, show us what to do." I knew I was not going to pay $115,000 for a new BMW, but I also knew that God can do amazing things. Drenda and I did not tell anyone about the car or mention to anyone that we were looking for a car.

About two weeks later, Drenda's brother called us and said, "I found Drenda's car!" "What do you mean you found Drenda's car?" I said. He said, "I saw this car for sale, and all of a sudden, I just felt that this was supposed to be Drenda's

CHAPTER THREE: How Do We Get Faith?

car, and I was supposed to tell you about it." "What kind of car is it?" I asked. "It is a BMW 645Ci, and it is perfect; I mean perfect. It is a couple of years old, low mileage, and there is not a scratch on it. It is perfect. Besides that, you know the man who is selling it." "I do?" I said. "Yes, he said. You should call him about it." Well, when he told me the car's make and model, knowing that it was the exact car that Drenda and I both had said we liked just a couple of weeks previously, I knew that God was up to something.

I called the man who owned the car. Yes, I did know him, and we talked a bit about the car, and he was telling me how great of a shape the car was in. And then he said these words to me. "You know, ever since we have been on the phone speaking about this car, I just really feel like this is supposed to be Drenda's car." I had not even mentioned to him that I was looking at the car for Drenda. The man went on and said, "I tell you what I am going to do. I am going to sell it to you for $28,000." I could hardly believe what my ears were hearing. The car was worth so much more than that. When I told Drenda about it, she was thrilled, to say the least.

We paid cash for that car and still have it today. It still runs and looks great. There is still not a scratch on it, and we have taken many drives in that car with the top down, the stereo blaring, and the sun breathing life into a tired day.

Our favorite trip was driving that awesome convertible through the Colorado mountains, with our camping supplies in the trunk. Our daughter Kirsten was with us on that trip, and I remember driving through Kansas on I-70 during the night with the top down. Kirsten was lying in the back asleep as I drove. The stars shone so brightly over our heads, and the road was vacant except for an occasional truck or two. It was one of those perfect nights where the air was just right and all was wonderful in the world. We spent the next two weeks driving through the Rockies, and I found out just how great that car handled. One word can describe it—awesome!

CHAPTER THREE: How Do We Get Faith?

But here is the one million-dollar question. How did that car get here? Why was it the exact car that Drenda said, "That's it!" about? I knew that the Kingdom of God brought that car into our lives. I knew that when I sowed that car to that pastor, I was putting spiritual law into place. I remember saying that I was receiving back a car, not an SUV, not a jeep—a car. I remember saying a nice one. But Drenda and I had to put the sickle in. That car would not have shown up until we said, "That's it!" Although I was in faith when I released that car, we had not put the sickle in until Drenda said, "That's it."

Another incident happened that brought out this principle in an even greater way. I like to hunt. I live in some very good hunting country, and I am blessed to own my own hunting land. On my 60 acres, I have about 19 acres of hardwoods and about 10 acres of marsh. I hunt deer and squirrel every year with great success. There are always ducks and geese flying around, but for some reason, I never really thought about hunting them. Oh, once or twice over the years, the boys and I walked down to the marsh and jumped up a few geese for supper. But we never truly duck hunted.

Well, a few years ago, as I watched dozens and dozens of ducks flying into the marsh, I thought that I would try some duck hunting. Wow, it was so exciting! I was hooked. During that fall's duck hunting, I found out that I needed some serious practice shooting at ducks. I managed to bag a few and found that they were very good to eat as well.

I noticed that many times the ducks were just out of range or on the edge of my shotgun's range, which I believed contributed to some of my misses. I was using my regular, all-around shotgun that I used for everything from rabbits to deer, a Remington model 11-87. Don't misunderstand. I love that gun, and it is a great gun. But I had heard there were new gun models that were made just for duck hunting. They were camouflaged and were chambered for three and a half inch magnum shells, which I knew would help on those long passing shots. I planned to look into one of

CHAPTER THREE: How Do We Get Faith?

them before the next duck season began.

Well, the duck season was over, it was then January, and I was walking through Cabela's and thought I would walk through the shotgun section to see what those guns looked like. As I walked into the shotgun section, I saw that they had a whole section dedicated to just shotguns for duck hunting. I looked at a few of them and thought about buying the one I liked, but it was $2,000 and the duck hunting season was months away. *I'll wait*, I thought to myself. But I did something unusual as I was about to leave. I really did not realize what I was doing when I did it. I just did it without thinking. I pointed at the shotgun I wanted and said out loud. "I'll have that gun, in the name of Jesus." Again, I did not think much about it; I was just making a declaration that I was going to have that gun. My heart had a clear picture of the duck gun I wanted.

I was invited to speak at a business conference a couple of weeks later, and something happened there that caught my attention.

After I spoke, the owner of the company walked up and said they had wanted to get me a gift in appreciation of my coming. He said, "We knew you like to hunt, so we bought you this shotgun." I was in shock as they brought out a brand-new, Benelli, semiautomatic duck gun, the exact one I had seen in the store, the one to which I had pointed! Are you seeing this? How did that exact gun show up? I had given dozens of guns away over the years but had never put in the sickle. In other words, I had sown those guns in faith and generosity but had never put in the sickle. I had never said, "Lord, that's it! That's the one I want." But the minute I did, the harvest showed up!

I was relating the story of the shotgun to a fellow minister friend of mine. He said, "Yes, I suppose God does that sometimes. He will just bless you with a special little gift to tell you He loves you." As I thought about what he said, I realized, "No, that is not right. Yes, God loves me, but He did not just want to surprise me with a little gift." The car and the gun had not come because God just wanted to show me He

CHAPTER THREE: How Do We Get Faith?

loved me. He showed me He loved me when He sent Jesus for me and gave me the Kingdom!

I have said for years that the church has done a fairly good job of teaching about giving but a horrible job of teaching people how to harvest. So can you tell what the sickle is from the preceding stories? I hope it is obvious! The sickle is our words!

> *The tongue has the power of life and death, and those who love it will eat its fruit.*
> —Proverb 18:21

There was a season where the church seemed to teach a lot about our confession. I have been with people, and you may have also, that would say something and then cover their mouths and say, "I need to watch my confession." That sounds like a noble task, and I agree that will help keep the Word in your heart. However, watching your confession really has nothing to do with the sickle. *What? But I thought you just said the sickle was our words.* Yes, I did, but just mastering the formula of saying the right thing is not the key by itself.

> *Truly, I say to you, whoever **<u>says</u>** to this mountain, "Be taken up and thrown into the sea," and does not doubt in his heart, but **<u>believes</u>** that what **<u>he says</u>** will come to pass, it will be done for him.*
> —Mark 11:23 (ESV)

Again, the sickle in Mark chapter 4 is your words! By the time Mark chapter 4 discusses the sickle, it has already discussed the process of faith and how to get it. It says when the seed is mature, you put in the sickle because the harvest has come. The harvest has come because you are in faith, agreeing with heaven in your heart. The above verse in Mark 11 bears out the same principle. Your heart believes the Word, then you speak and release heaven's authority. But notice the phrase, *"believes that what he says will come to pass."*

The test of faith is if *you* believe what you are saying.

CHAPTER THREE: How Do We Get Faith?

Just saying or confessing the Word of God is not faith by itself. Unless your heart is in agreement with heaven, you can confess until you are blue in the face and nothing will happen.

So should you monitor your confession or your heart?

> *The good person brings what is good out of the good stored up in his heart, and the evil person brings what is evil out of the evil within. To be sure, what his mouth speaks flows from the heart.*
> —Luke 6:45 (EHV)

> *Above all else, guard your heart, for everything you do flows from it. Keep your mouth free of perversity; keep corrupt talk far from your lips.*
> —Proverbs 4:23-24

We can clearly see that what we say comes out of our hearts and what our hearts believe. By following the process in Mark chapter 4, we know how to actually change what our hearts believe and bring them into alignment with heaven and in faith. Then when we are fully persuaded, we put the sickle in with our words and action. Got it? Great! Let's move on.

As we continue our discussion on faith, I want to bring up a question that you must be able to answer.

CHAPTER FOUR
HOW DO YOU KNOW IF YOU ARE ACTUALLY IN FAITH?

That is a great question and one you **must** know since it is impossible to pray the prayer of faith without first being *in* faith. There are many ways to know if you are in faith or not, many symptoms that you need to know and to look for. You can make a lot of bad fear-based decisions when you are not in faith. Fear-based decisions will always hold you hostage to the earth curse and will cause you to miss out on what God wants for you.

So what is the evidence of being in faith? The first sign is easy; you can look back at our definition of faith and understand that being fully persuaded in your heart is a real key. But many times, we think we are persuaded but are only agreeing in our *minds* with the Word and not with our hearts. You need to be able to tell the difference. When you are fully persuaded, there is, of course, a mental agreement with what the Word says, but also there is a knowing, being sure, a confidence that brings peace and expectation.

CHAPTER FOUR: How Do You Know If You Are Actually *in* Faith?

> *Faith is being sure about what we hope for, convinced about things we do not see.*
> —Hebrews 11:1 (EHV)

If you had evidence that you had something, would you still need to be reassured that you had it? Of course not. Again, when you are in faith, there is a knowing, a peace, and a confidence that you have what the Word of God says, even though you may not see it yet. Many people say it this way: "I know that I know that I know that I know I have it." This knowing is from the inside and not from what circumstances are telling you. It is in your spirit man, or your heart. Fear is gone, and there are no more nagging thoughts of worry bombarding your mind; you know it is done.

Another aspect of being in faith is joy and expectation. Your answer is here. You have it! Faith is more than a feeling of peace or confidence, although you will have that. You should also be able to defend your position spiritually. When I say that, think of a courtroom and you as the attorney cross-examining the witness. Why do you believe what you believe about your situation? How would you defend your position? There is only one answer: the Word of God.

For instance, if someone came to your house and said, "Hey, get out of my house," would you say, "Oh, I am sorry; give us a day, and we will be out"? No, you wouldn't! You would probably laugh at them. If the fellow said, "No, this is my house; get out or I will see you in court," your reply would be, "I will gladly see you in court!" At the hearing, you would calmly show the judge your deed. He would take one look at it and arrest the other guy for harassment and make him pay all court costs. Your confidence was established not on how you felt and your emotions but rather on the law and the fact that you legally owned the house.

When it comes to being in faith, I find that, many times, people who do not understand what faith is are easily confused and putting their confidence in their *actions* instead of their only source of faith, which is the Word of God.

CHAPTER FOUR: How Do You Know If You Are Actually *in* Faith?

It is easy to confuse the action or formula of acting on the Word of God with the real power of the Kingdom, which comes from a heart that is confidently persuaded.

For instance, if you sowed money into the Kingdom of God, and I asked you why you believe you will receive a return on that giving, your answer should not be, "Because on such and such a date, I gave a certain amount of money." That confession is looking only at your action, the formula, and has no anchor of assurance. Your assurance can only come from the Word of God.

I can't count the number of people I have prayed with that when asked why they believe they will receive when I pray simply stare at me with no answer. When I ask, I am looking for their faith, their agreement with heaven. I want to hear them say, "I know I will receive because God has promised me in such and such book of the Bible and in such and such verse that it is mine." Chances are if they can't give me a Scripture, they are not anchored and they really do not have a clue where their boat is going.

Remember, faith can only exist when you know the will of God. Why? Because faith can only exist when your heart is in agreement with the will of God.

I believe that many people think they are in faith when they are not. Again, their minds may agree that the Word of God is true and good, but faith is there only when their hearts are fully persuaded. For many, their minds agree with the Word of God, but their hearts are not settled.

Here is a good illustration of what I am talking about, and I believe it will point out that many are not in faith when they think they are. What if I were to tell you that I had recently found out that the sky was not blue, as people said, but that the color blue as they called it was really the color yellow? In other words, I told you that we had been taught wrong all our lives about colors and that blue is not really blue but

CHAPTER FOUR: How Do You Know If You Are Actually *in* Faith?

yellow. What would you do? Would you gasp in shock and quickly grab your cell phone and call your first grade teacher and yell at them, accusing them of messing up your life, teaching you all the colors wrong? I do not think so. There would be no emotional reaction of fear, no drama. You would simply know that I was an idiot, dismiss the comment as irrational, and go about your business. Why? Because you are fully persuaded that blue is blue!

Now, let's compare my example to our faith discussion. What if you were fully persuaded of what God said about healing, and a doctor told you that you were going to die of cancer? You would look at that doctor and think he was the idiot because you knew there was no way that could happen. Why? It's because you were fully persuaded of the healing provisions that Jesus paid for. Do you see it?

Of course, many people pray, but upon examination, I find their prayers are not prayers of faith but of *hope*, with them unsure of the outcome. My friend, this is why it is so important that we build ourselves up with the Word of God. We need to know what God's will is so that we can be confident in what He says, and also so we can reject what is not His will.

Let me give you an example from my own life that illustrates just how important it is to feed on what God says about life.

I was tired, as it had been a tough few weeks as a business owner (this was before I pastored a church). My schedule had been packed with sales calls and, of course, the financial pressure of living on commissions. I was going to my dentist for a routine filling. Everything was normal until the dentist went to inject the Novocain. As he inserted the needle, there was a sudden jolt, and then my jaw instantly went numb, as opposed to it slowly numbing up. I was surprised, and I told the dentist what had happened. He said, "Oh, I guess I hit the nerve." I quickly asked him, "Is that normal?" He said these words, "Well, it usually heals up."

What? Did I hear him correctly? "Doctor, what do

CHAPTER FOUR: How Do You Know If You Are Actually *in* Faith?

you mean it usually heals up?" I asked. He said, "Well, about 80 percent to 85 percent of the time, it completely heals up with no permanent negative effect."

What? Suddenly fear rose up in me. *Now what? Is it going to heal up?* My mind was starting to be consumed with fearful thoughts. After my appointment, my face stayed numb, unlike a normal dentist's appointment where the numbness slowly wears off. I was heading to a client's appointment about an hour away from the dentist's appointment, so I had plenty of time to think about what had just happened. But all the way to that appointment, I was in agony, not from any pain but from the lack of peace and from the fear that was swirling through my mind.

On the way home from the appointment, later in the day, I stopped at a friend's house. My face was still numb, and I was looking for some reassurance from someone that this thing would heal up. Notice my mistake: I did not look to the Word of God but to a person who was not even a strong believer for my confidence. I told this person what had happened and was waiting for their, "That's no big deal, Gary; it will heal up!" Instead, here is what I heard. "Oh, no! I had a friend who had that happen, and their face never healed. Their face has been paralyzed ever since." I could not believe what I was hearing! My mind was then in fear overdrive. I acted like I knew it would be okay and thanked him for his time.

In desperation, I stopped by another friend's home and asked the same question, and, in shock, I heard the same reply, "Oh, no," they said, "I had a friend who had this happen, and their face never healed. Their face is still paralyzed today."

After this visit, I was undone. I knew that God heals (in my mind), but I just could not get rid of that fear. My heart was definitely not persuaded. That night, I was in agony! My mind was full of fear, and my face was still just as numb as it had been at the dentist's office. As I was trying to get to sleep, I began to feel a

CHAPTER FOUR: How Do You Know If You Are Actually *in* Faith?

bit of pain under my right ear. Could it be? My dad had fought a battle with Bell's palsy a year or two earlier, and he had told me that it had started with some pain just under his ear. Bell's palsy occurs when the nerve that controls the facial muscles, which travels through a small hole in the bone just under the ear, becomes pinched by an infection or inflammation.

As I lay there trying to find sleep, all I could hear were these words going through my thoughts, *You are going to have Bell's palsy just like your dad.* When I woke up in the morning, I had a full-blown case of Bell's palsy! Not only was my jaw numb, but also my entire face on the right side was numb, and I could not close my eyes or my mouth. I was a mess.

I went to a local doctor to confirm my suspicions. After the examination, he looked at me and said that I indeed had a full-blown case of Bell's palsy. I then said, "What happens next?" He said, "Well, in about 80 to 85 percent of the cases, it will heal up without permanent paralysis." *Did he say what I thought he just said?*

At that point, I knew that I was in trouble. I knew that the devil would not stop there, and I did not want to see what came next. I knew enough about spiritual warfare to realize I was heading in the wrong direction. Remember, this was years ago before I knew very much about these types of things. But I knew enough to realize that I had to tackle this thing spiritually if I was going to have any success at beating it. I also realized that this was a demonic setup to catch me off guard when I was tired and not anticipating any trouble.

At that point, I knew that my only hope was the Word of God. In myself, I had absolutely no ability to stop the fear that was plaguing my mind. So I wrote out 3x5 cards with healing Scriptures on them and posted them all over my house. I repented before the Lord and began the process of developing faith in my heart. I knew that I had to sow the Word in my heart for faith to develop, so I would meditate on the Word of God throughout the day.

At first, nothing changed. My face stayed numb,

CHAPTER FOUR: How Do You Know If You Are Actually *in* Faith?

and I constantly fought the spirit of fear. After about a week, with still nothing changing in my face, it happened!

Just like the process our Scripture in Mark 4:26-28 teaches, as I sowed the Word into my heart, faith began to be formed: first the blade, then the stalk, then the head, and then the mature grain in the head.

Throughout this entire process, there was not agreement and thus no faith—yet. However, even though I did not see change or know how this process works, according to our Scripture in Mark 4, things were indeed changing.

The change I am talking about is not manifested in the natural realm yet, but the change is occurring in our hearts. If we hold on to the Word, the Word slowly changes our hearts' belief system from one of unbelief to agreement with heaven all by itself.

So in this case, I held on to the Word, knowing that it was my only answer. Suddenly, one day, as I was walking through my house with all those 3x5 cards with healing Scriptures on them posted everywhere, I just happened to glance at one that I had seen a hundred times. But this time when I looked at it, BAM! Suddenly, the anointing came on me, fear instantly left, and I KNEW that I was healed. Yes, my face was still numb. There was no change, but I *knew* I was healed. Within a couple of hours, my face was completely normal, with all the numbness gone. Praise God! The Word works!

Even though I had allowed my spiritual life to weaken due to my neglect and busyness, I eventually realized my mistake and repented from my foolishness. This was way back when I was first learning how faith really worked, and I did not have a lot of experience in this area. I look back on what I did, asking people of my future when in trouble instead of going straight to the Word of God, as foolish. Once I understood what was going on, I did turn to the Word of God with confidence.

Unfortunately, most people are not confident

CHAPTER FOUR: How Do You Know If You Are Actually *in* Faith?

in this process because they have never been taught about faith and how it comes. Since they are unaware of the process, when they are under pressure, they let go of the Word, thinking it does not work.

CHAPTER FIVE
UNDERSTAND SATAN'S COUNTERATTACK

Christine came to our church not knowing much about God. She was born again in one of our Sunday morning services, and her life was radically changed. In our church, we have a Kingdom orientation class. One of the areas we talk and teach about is the legal right to receive healing. Christine had been having trouble with her hearing for years. In fact, she had been wearing a hearing aid for 40 years and had already lost over 50 percent of her hearing. Her mother was deaf, and her brother was also suffering from this same issue with loss of hearing. When Christine heard that, as a believer, she had a legal right to be healed, she was so excited!

In the class, my wife, Drenda, laid her hands on her and prayed for her hearing to be open, and instantly, pop, she could hear perfectly. Christine began screaming and crying and praising God. When Drenda and Christine came and told me the good news, I felt an urge to warn her about Satan's counterattack. I told Drenda to instruct Christine that if the symptoms started to come back for her to

CHAPTER FIVE: Understand Satan's Counterattack

speak boldly to the issue and declare that she was healed and for Satan to back off.

The next morning, the test came. Her hearing had reverted back to her inability to hear well. So, she did exactly what we said, "NO! Satan, I am not receiving this. I am healed, and I *was* healed, in the name of Jesus!" Pop! Her ears popped open, and they have stayed open ever since.

Remember that Satan will counterattack and try to retake territory. Don't let him do it. Stand on the Word of God!

In this short book, I have taken some time to give you a basic understanding of what faith is, how it functions, how to know if you are in faith, and where to get faith. For the Kingdom of God to operate in your life, you *have* to know this.

Remember, Jesus told the woman who received her healing in Matthew 9:20-22, *"Your faith has healed you."* And so shall it be for you: Your faith—your heart being fully convinced of

DOING FAITH RIGHT

what heaven says, and putting in the sickle—will be your answer for any problem or need you may face in life.

ABOUT THE AUTHOR

Gary Keesee is a television host, author, international speaker, financial expert, successful entrepreneur, and pastor who has made it his mission to help people win in life, especially in the areas of faith, family, and finances.

After years of living in poverty, Gary and his wife, Drenda, discovered the principles of the Kingdom of God, and their lives were drastically changed. Together, under the direction of the Holy Spirit, they created several successful businesses and paid off all of their debt. Now, they spend their time declaring the Good News of the Kingdom of God around the world through Faith Life Now, their organization that exists to motivate, educate, and inspire people from all walks of life and backgrounds to pursue success, walk out their God-designed purposes, and leave positive spiritual and moral legacies for their families.

Faith Life Now produces two television programs—*Fixing the Money Thing* and *Drenda*—as well as practical resources and conferences. Gary and Drenda also speak at events around the world.

Gary is also the president and founder of Forward Financial Group and the founding pastor of Faith Life Church, which has campuses in New Albany and Powell, Ohio.

Gary and Drenda, their five adult children and their spouses, and their grandchildren all reside in Central Ohio.

For additional resources by both Gary and Drenda, visit faithlifenow.com.

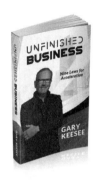

Get ready to discover how to accelerate your success and reach your dreams!

Did you know that over 80% of Americans don't like their jobs? So, why do they keep getting up each morning to go to a job that they hate? Because paying the bills has replaced their vision. Debt has hijacked their freedom and caused them to give up on their dreams.

Unfinished Business: Nine Laws for Acceleration puts everything on the table and walks you through the steps to change your mindset—your thinking—to one of opportunity and acceleration, so you don't leave any of your dreams, your impact, or your God-designed destiny unfinished.

With his combination of practical insights, stories, and Scriptures, Gary Keesee walks you through the simple steps to go from just surviving to thriving.

With over 30 years of experience, Gary has helped countless people realize their God-given dreams and purposes. He wants to help you win in life, take territory, and make sure that you leave no unfinished business behind.

Get you copy of *Unfinished Business* by going to faithlifenow.com